THE DIVINE KINGSHIP
OF THE
SHILLUK OF THE NILOTIC SUDAN

T0346180

THE DIVINE KINGSHIP

OF THE

SHILLUK OF THE NILOTIC SUDAN

BY

E. E. EVANS-PRITCHARD

*Professor of Social Anthropology and
Fellow of All Souls College,
Oxford*

THE FRAZER LECTURE 1948

CAMBRIDGE
AT THE UNIVERSITY PRESS
1948

CAMBRIDGE
UNIVERSITY PRESS

University Printing House, Cambridge CB2 8BS, United Kingdom

Published in the United States of America by Cambridge University Press, New York

Cambridge University Press is part of the University of Cambridge.

It furthers the University's mission by disseminating knowledge in the pursuit of education, learning and research at the highest international levels of excellence.

www.cambridge.org
Information on this title: www.cambridge.org/9781107678439

© Cambridge University Press 1948

First published 1948
Re-issued 2014

A catalogue record for this publication is available from the British Library

ISBN 978-1-107-67843-9 Paperback

INTRODUCTION

THE central theme of *The Golden Bough* was the divine kingship, and it has seemed to me appropriate that a lecture established in its author's honour and now dedicated to his memory should be on that subject. I propose, therefore, to examine one of the examples of divine kingship cited by Sir James Frazer, that of the Shilluk of the Anglo-Egyptian Sudan, and to discuss it as a problem of social structure.

It was recorded as early as 1905 that it was a Shilluk custom to kill their kings[1] and much information about the Shilluk kingship in general has since been collected. Professor and Mrs Seligman studied the institution in 1909-10 and it was they who brought it to the notice of Sir James Frazer and into the main stream of ethnological theory. Apart from the writings of the Seligmans and a number of articles by other hands there are two monographs on the Shilluk, *The*

[1] Banholzer, P. and Giffen, J. K., *The Anglo-Egyptian Sudan* (edited by Count Gleichen, 1905), ch. VIII, p. 199.

1

Shilluk People by Professor Diedrich Westermann, who conducted linguistic research among the Shilluk in 1910, and Father Wilhelm Hofmayr's *Die Schilluk*, largely based on the observations of Father Banholzer and other of his fellow Catholic missionaries, which date from the beginning of the century. Father Hofmayr himself worked among the Shilluk from 1906 to 1916. There has, indeed, long been a considerable body of knowledge about the Shilluk and I would not have considered it profitable to discuss the Shilluk kingship afresh were it not that new light has recently been shed on their social structure, and more particularly on the place of the kingship in it, by officers of the Sudan Political Service. It is significant that two of them studied anthropology before joining the Sudan Service, Mr P. P. Howell at Cambridge, from where he had carried out some research among the Shilluk before joining the Service, and Mr W. P. G. Thomson at Oxford. It is from this literature, and especially from the more recent accounts, that I have drawn the material for my lecture, for though the Shilluk live in a part of the world with which I am very familiar, my contact with them has been slight.

The Shilluk are the most northern of the Nilotic peoples and have been for centuries in contact

2

with the Arab population of the northern Sudan. Their country was first subjected to intermittent taxation and raiding by the Turks about 1820 and was finally conquered by them in 1867 and became part of the Ottoman Empire. When the Turkish Administration succumbed to the Sudanese Mahdi the Shilluk were involved in a struggle against this new ruler and afterwards against his Khalifa. Lord Kitchener arrived in Shillukland at the end of 1898 and since that time the people have been under Anglo-Egyptian administration. I mention these political events because they have strongly influenced the Shilluk kingship for close on a century, during which the kings have been executed, exiled, deposed, and nominated, by foreign governments. The funerary rites of a dead king and the procedures of election and investiture of a new king were probably not performed in the full traditional manner during this period.

SOCIAL STRUCTURE

The hamlets of the Shilluk, who number about 110,000 souls, are almost continuous, like beads on a string, along the west bank of the Nile from near Lake No to about lat. 12 N. with a number of settlements on the east bank and along the lower reaches of the Sobat. Their country is treeless savannah but, unlike their cousins the Nuer and Dinka, they are predominantly agricultural and sedentary, for their long river frontage gives them adequate water and grazing in the dry season for the comparatively few cattle (about 25,000) they possess.[1] The brief account I give of their social structure is mostly derived from articles in *Sudan Notes and Records* by Mr Pumphrey and Mr Howell.[2]

The hamlets (*myer*, sing. *pac*), built from 100 yards to a mile or so apart on high ground parallel to the river, vary in size from one to fifty homesteads; a homestead (*gol*), the residence of a family (*gol*), consisting usually of two huts encircled by a fence. Each hamlet is occupied by members of an extended family, or small lineage, with their wives, and the homesteads of this group are arranged in a rough horseshoe shape around a common cattle-byre, which shelters the animals in the rains and is used as a club at all seasons, and a common kraal. The headman of a hamlet (*jal dwong pac*) who is also the head of a lineage in

[1] I am indebted to Mr John Donald of the Sudan Political Service for the most recent figures of human and bovine population.
[2] M. E. C. Pumphrey, 'The Shilluk Tribe', *S.N. and R.* (1941); P. P. Howell, 'The Shilluk Settlement', *ibid.* (1941).

the settlement of which it forms part represents the hamlet on the council of the settlement and receives in consequence a robe of honour from the king or from the chief of the settlement. If his hamlet is only a subsidiary seat of a lineage in the settlement he is regarded merely as its senior member.

The settlement to which I have just referred is called *podh*, a word which has a number of meanings but generally designates a group of hamlets, occupied by different lineages, which, though there may be much competition between them, unite for defence, for the ritual of age-sets (an institution otherwise of little political importance), and in intersettlement and national affairs, and have a common chief. There are about a hundred of these settlements in Shillukland, each having a population of from less than 100 to more than 600 adult males. They are structurally distinct groups of a political kind though the distance that divides a settlement from adjacent settlements may be no greater than that which separates a hamlet from its nearest neighbours in the same settlement.

In every settlement there is a dominant lineage, the *dyil*, the owners of the soil, with whom the various stranger and immigrant accretions (*wedh*) identify themselves politically and with whom they form a separate social community with its own corporate life. This lineage is generally dominant in numbers as well as in virtue of the prestige derived from its traditional association with the settlement site. The chief of the settlement is chosen from it and by its members, though the stranger lineages have some say in the election, which must be confirmed by the king (*reth*) of the Shilluk. Even when a stranger lineage, sometimes a branch of the royal clan (*kwareth*), becomes more numerous in a settlement than its dominant lineage and dispossesses its members of the chieftainship they still retain some prestige as owners of the soil. Unity in a settlement and the authority of its chief are said to depend on its integration around a powerful dominant lineage. I must, therefore, say something here about Shilluk lineages.

There has been, and still is, some obscurity about Shilluk descent groups. There are said to be in Shillukland about 100 groups designated by the word *kwa* (descendants) followed by the name of the ancestor of the group. These are often described in the literature as exogamous clans but many of them might perhaps be better spoken of as lineages. They have a typical lineage structure with its characteristic branching off in response to the formation of new territorial units. Colonies of the same lineage are found in several settlements, so that in any settlement several different descent groups are represented, one of them, as I have already explained, being always dominant in it and identified with the settlement politically. Although the dispersed lineages of a clan do not intermarry, and sometimes acknowledge their common descent in other ways, a man generally thinks in terms of his localized lineage, reference being usually to the ancestor who founded the lineage in his settlement. It is interesting to note a further common feature of lineage systems: the descendants of a man who has settled with his wife's people trace their descent through the wife to the lineage in whose home they live. This practice is, as among the other Nilotic peoples, one of the ways in which stranger lineages are grafted into the genealogical structure of the dominant lineage in a settlement. However, until we know more than we do at present about the distribution of lineages, about their genealogical structure, and about the part they play in intersettlement relations it will not be possible to estimate fully their political significance.

All the Shilluk settlements compose a common polity, the kingdom of Shillukland. They are

7

segments of an organization. It seems that in pre-Turkish times there was a tendency for contiguous settlements to combine for war against other settlements or under the leadership of an outstanding personality, but such combinations were not permanent, or even consistent enough for us to speak of them as political groups. The Turkish Administration tried to give greater consistency to them so that they could be used as administrative units, and the Anglo-Egyptian Government has done the same and calls them divisions and appoints a chief for each. Previously they appear to have been little more than districts or localities, and the only chiefs between the king and the chiefs of settlements were those of Ger, northern Shilluk-land, and Luak, southern Shillukland, whose functions had, as we shall see, a ritual rather than an administrative character, and those of Muomo and Tonga, the settlements which are the northern and southern marches of Shillukland, whose functions were also partly ritual. In Shilluk speech Muomo and Tonga correspond exactly, Professor Westermann tells us, to the expression of the ancient Hebrews: from Dan unto Beersheba.[1]

[1] Diedrich Westermann, *The Shilluk People. Their Language and Folklore* (1912), p. xx.

8

Northern Shillukland and southern Shillukland are the arches of the politico-religious kingdom of the Shilluk of which the kingship is the keystone. That segmentation has taken this particular form is doubtless due to the peculiar ribbon-distribution of the Shilluk settlements.

The whole Shilluk people recognize a single head and we can therefore speak of the Shilluk nation and of their king, and it is with his place in the national polity that this lecture is particularly concerned. According to Shilluk tradition the present king is the thirty-first of his line. All the kings are believed to be descended from Nyikang, the leader of the Shilluk in their heroic age, who led them into their present homeland, conquering it from its inhabitants and dividing it among the lineages of his followers; and Nyikang, or, as we would say, the spirit of Nyikang, is believed to be in every king and to have passed from king to king down the line of his successors. Nyikang is thus a mythological personification of the timeless kingship which itself symbolizes the national structure, a changeless moral order.

The rule of succession is that only a son of a king can be invested with the kingship. As many sons of kings have never succeeded to the throne, there are to-day numerous and widely diffused branches of the royal clan whose members are ineligible for royal office and lack authority, unless they are also chiefs of settlements, although they are treated with deference by commoners in virtue of their descent. Indeed, the royal clan is easily the largest single clan in the whole country, being said to comprise perhaps a fifteenth of the nation. In some areas its members are more numerous than commoners and have supplanted commoner lineages in the chieftainship of settlements. This process, which continues to-day, has been going on for a long time, for it is said that Abudok, the eighth ruler (and only queen) of the Shilluk, prophesied that one day the royal clan would eat up the rest of the Shilluk.[1] It results from the custom of sending pregnant wives of a king from the royal capital to bear their children in other, generally their natal, settlements. Their daughters are not allowed to marry and therefore do not start lines of descent which would count as sisters' sons to the royal house. Their sons are brought up by settlement chiefs, often their mothers' brothers, and not in the capital. When a prince (*nyireth*) marries he builds a separate hamlet near that of the settlement chief

[1] Westermann, *op. cit*. p. 149.

who has reared him and there his descendants live. Some lineages of the royal clan, the *ororo*, have been formally deprived of their noble status and can now intermarry with their parent clan. They are said to be descendants of Ocolo, the fifth king, who were degraded by his successor, but Father Hofmayr's and Father Crazzolara's accounts[1] would suggest that some of them may be descended from nobles degraded by other kings, and further research will probably confirm this. They are few in number but they hold the important chieftainship of Tonga settlement and they play a leading part in the royal funerary and investiture rites. A king always has some of their daughters among his wives and it is said to be their duty to smother him in certain circumstances.

The emergence of what may be called aristocratic status has been accompanied by the formation of numerous groups of persons of the category of *bang reth*, royal clients. They are descendants of retainers of past kings—captured enemies, certain homicides, persons who have become possessed by the spirit of Nyikang, and poor men who have

[1] Wilhelm Hofmayr, *Die Schilluk* (1925), pp. 66, 83, and 261–2; P. J. P. Crazzolara, 'Beiträge zur Kenntnis der Religion und Zauberei bei den Schilluk', *Anthropos* (1932), p. 185.

attached themselves to the court—and have been given the fictional collectivity of exogamous lineages. They are said to be rather more numerous than the royal clan. During a king's lifetime his special band of retainers used, until the practice was discouraged by the Government, to live near the capital in a hamlet of their own, but when their master was buried in his natal settlement some of them moved there with his elderly widows, and their descendants remained there to tend his shrine. Also, when a prince was 'planted out', as the Shilluk say, in a settlement, his father sent some of his retainers to live there and these became *bang nyireth*, a prince's clients. They served the prince during his lifetime, and after his death their descendants continued to live near the prince's descendants as a fictitious lineage. Consequently, where there is a branch of the royal clan in a settlement there is usually a lineage of clients in the same settlement. The clients are merged in the general category of commoners, *colo*, of which word 'Shilluk' is an Arabic corruption, though it is said of them that they have a slightly lower social status than members of other commoner clans because they have no traditional rights in the settlements in which they live.

12

The development of the Shilluk kingship has thus produced, though not in a very pronounced or rigid form, a social hierarchy of royal house, nobility (other members of the royal clan), and commoners (including persons of client origin).

THE KINGSHIP

If we are to understand the place of the kingship in Shilluk society we must, I think, beware of attempts to define it in terms of judicial and administrative functions and view it rather as a ritual office and in a wider political context. In 1903 Father Tappi wrote that the authority of the king is 'absolute'.[1] Professor and Mrs Seligman have described the king as 'absolute head—temporal and spiritual—of a state whose territory is divided into a number of provinces, each administered by a chief directly responsible to the sovereign and acting as his proxy',[2] and Professor Westermann has also written of the power of the king as 'absolute'.[3] Father Hofmayr says that 'Mit dem Regierungsantritt ist der König Herr des Landes, das er nach Belieben vergeben

[1] P. C. Tappi, 'Notes Ethnologiques sur les Chillouks', *Bull. Soc. Khediv. de Géog.* (1903), p. 122.
[2] *Pagan Tribes of the Nilotic Sudan* (1932), p. 39.
[3] *Op. cit.* p. xlvii.

kann, und Herr sogar des Eigentums seiner Unter-
tanen'.[1] These statements would seem to require
some modification. As Mr Pumphrey has pointed
out, it is unlikely that the so-called 'provinces' were
in fact more than districts or that they were in any
sense administrative departments before they were
made into something of the kind by foreign governments.[2] Moreover, though doubtless the king exer-
cised considerable influence in the country and may
have confirmed settlement chiefs in office, he did not
nominate them. They were heads of settlements in
virtue of their position as heads of lineages dominant
in those settlements and although they had certain
duties to the king it is, I think, wrong to describe
them as being in any sense administrative officials.
To use such terms as 'state', 'government', and
'administration' in speaking of the Shilluk political
system would appear to me, in the light of what is
now known of it, to be a mistake.

It is true that the more recent authorities imply
rather than explicitly state what in their opinion
is the position of the king. Mr Howell and Mr
Thomson speak of 'the theoretical omnipotence'
of the king and of a 'theoretically omnipotent

---

[1] *Op. cit.* pp. 150–1.
[2] *Op. cit.* pp. 18–19.

monarchy'.[1] Mr Pumphrey says that in the old days 'justice was probably rough and large-scale fighting more prevalent than litigation'.[2] Indeed, feuds appear to have been rampant in the past, and it is not very clear how they were composed. We are told that major disputes were sometimes brought before the king, but he can hardly be said to have tried such cases. If he intervened at all it was to support partially one side to a quarrel. We are told that when a settlement waged 'unjustifiable' war on another or refused persistently to listen to the king he might raise a 'royal levy' from the adjacent settlements and with this force and his own retainers raid the recalcitrants, seizing their cattle and burning their homesteads. He kept some of the cattle for himself and the rest were taken by those who supported his action. The raiding force would generally be strong enough to discourage resistance.[3] Compensation for injury seems, therefore, to have been obtained by self-help, sometimes backed by royal intervention. Without confirmation I am not inclined to accept Father Hofmayr's statement that compensation for homicide was

[1] Howell, *op. cit.* p. 57; P. P. Howell and W. P. G. Thomson, 'The Death of a Reth of the Shilluk and the Installation of his Successor', *S.N. and R.* (1946), p. 8.
[2] *Op. cit.* p. 19.   [3] *Ibid.* p. 12.

paid to the king alone.[1] A different picture of the
king's part in the settlement of disputes is painted
by Mr Oyler of the American Mission, who wit-
nessed the settlement of a feud, which had been
going on in a district for more than three years, by
the joint intervention of the king and the Government. From his account it is evident that the king
could not have imposed a settlement had the dis-
putants not been ready to accept one, that the part
played in it by the king was that of peacemaker and
not of judge, and that his participation can better
be described as sacerdotal than as governmental.[2]
The king of the Shilluk reigns but does not govern.

The king's sacerdotal role in the settlement of
feuds gives us a clue to what is confirmed by a great
weight of further evidence: his sacral position in
Shilluk society. Our authorities, indeed, speak of
the king as the 'Hoherpriester des Landes',[3] of 'the
royal and priestly line' and of its 'priestly function',[4]
and of the king as 'the high priest of the tribal
religion'.[5] Both his functions and his status are
primarily of a ritual order. He makes sacrifices on

[1] *Op. cit.* p. 162.
[2] 'The Shilluk Peace Ceremony', *S.N. and* ⌐ (1920), pp. 296–9.
[3] Hofmayr, *op. cit.* p. 152.
[4] Banholzer and Giffen, *op. cit.* p. 197.
[5] Pumphrey, *op. cit.* p. 19.

important occasions, especially for rain and for victory in war, and it is his duty to provide cattle for the sacred herds of Nyikang at Nyilual and Wau and a canoe for Nyikang's shrine at Nyibodho. Nyikang, the culture hero of the Shilluk, their first king, and the creator of their nation, is immanent in him and this makes him the double pivot of Shilluk society, the political head of the nation and the centre of the national cult. The kingship is the common symbol of the Shilluk people and, Nyikang being immortal, an abiding institution which binds past and present and future generations.

The correspondence of political structure with religious cult can be seen at every point of the structure. The territorial segments of the nation and their association with lineages is, as we have noted, validated by the myth of Nyikang's parcelling out of his conquests among the clans, the strands of which are, moreover, caught up into a single mythological point, Nyikang. Some trace their descent from his companions, some from his collateral relatives, others from the original inhabitants of the country conquered by him, and yet others from men who played some part in his saga. The lineage heads who are the chiefs of settlements have ritual duties to the kingship: in

17

particular, ceremonial services at the king's investiture, the building of huts at Fashoda, which is both the royal capital and the cult centre of Nyikang, and the upkeep of Nyikang's other shrines and those of past kings. These shrines are widely distributed throughout the country so that every section of it participates in the cult of Nyikang, who is, it must be borne in mind, not only the semi-divine hero of Shilluk mythology but also the king at every period of their history. Indeed, the shrines of Nyikang, what Professor Seligman calls his cenotaphs, are indistinguishable from the tomb-shrines of dead kings and they have the same ceremonial functions in the life of the people: in the rain-making ceremonies, at harvest time, and in times of sickness and pestilence.[1] The religion and cosmogony of the Shilluk are bound up with the political system through the identification of Nyikang with the king. The kingship stands at the centre of Shilluk moral values.

We can only understand the place of the kingship in Shilluk society when we realize that it is not the individual at any time reigning who is king, but

[1] Prof. C. G. Seligman, 'The Cult of Nyakang and the Divine Kings of the Shilluk', *Report of the Wellcome Tropical Research Laboratories* (1911), pp. 221 and 225.

Nyikang who is the medium between man and God (*Juok*) and is believed in some way to participate in God as he does in the king. 'Nyikang is the *reth* but the *reth* is not Nyikang.'[1] The participation of Nyikang in the king raises the kingship to a plane above all sectional interests, whether local or of descent. All the Shilluk share in the kingship, however their loyalties may pull them apart in other matters, because in Nyikang are centred all those interests which are common to all the people: success in war against foreigners and the fertility and health of men, cattle, crops, and of those wild beasts which are of service to man. Professor Westermann tells us that 'everything they value most in their national and private life, has its origin in him'.[2] Mr Howell and Mr Thomson tell us that when a king dies the Shilluk say '*piny bugon*', 'there is no land'[3]—the centre of the Shilluks' world has fallen out. It is restored by the investiture of a new king, for though kings may perish the kingship, that is Nyikang, endures. Mr Oyler tells us: 'They say that if Nikawng should die, the whole Shilluk race would perish.'[4]

[1] Howell and Thomson, *op. cit.* p. 8. [2] *Op. cit.* p. xliii.
[3] Howell and Thomson, *op. cit.* p. 18.
[4] Rev. D. S. Oyler, 'Nikawng and the Shilluk Migration', *S.N. and R.* (1918), p. 115.

Because of the mystical values associated with the kingship and centred in the person of the king he must keep himself in a state of ritual purity, by performing certain actions and observing certain prescriptions, and in a state of physical perfection. Our authorities say that the Shilluk believe that should the king become physically weak the whole people might suffer, and, further, that if a king becomes sick or senile he should be killed to avoid some grave national misfortune, such as defeat in war, epidemic, or famine. The king must be killed to save the kingship and with it the whole Shilluk people.

This would seem to be the reasoning behind Shilluk statements that the king may be strangled, or suffocated, or walled up in a hut and left to die there, if he fails to satisfy his wives or shows signs of illness or senility. In view of the great importance Sir James Frazer and others have attached to these statements I must confess that I consider them of interest more as an indication of the mystical nature of the kingship than as evidence that the kings were, in fact, ever killed in the ways mentioned or for the reasons given. It is true that Professor and Mrs Seligman state categorically that 'there is not the least doubt that kings of the Shilluk were killed with due ceremony when they began to show signs of old age or ill health',[1] but I have failed to find convincing evidence that any Shilluk king was put to death in either circumstance, although some of the kings must have qualified long before they died for execution on the grounds alleged; and I am persuaded that the story of kings being walled up in a hut is a confusion arising from the usual walling up of the remains of a dead king, the bones being buried after decomposition of the flesh. In the absence of other than traditional evidence of royal executions in Shilluk history and in view of the contradictory accounts cited I conclude that the ceremonial putting to death of kings is probably a fiction. It possibly arises from the dual personality of the king, who is both himself and Nyikang, both an individual and an institution, which accounts also for the linguistic convention that a king does not die but disappears just as Nyikang is said not to have died but to have disappeared, in his case in a storm. I will return to this question of regicide after I have reviewed the procedures of election and investiture of kings to show what light they shed on the nature of the kingship.

[1] *Report of the Wellcome Tropical Research Laboratories,* p. 221; also *Pagan Tribes of the Nilotic Sudan,* pp. 90–2. Howell and Thomson say (*op. cit.* p. 19) that ceremonial strangulation is traditional for all members of the royal clan.

21

ROYAL ELECTION AND INVESTITURE

The phases of the investiture of a new king were excellently described by Mr P. Munro[1] of the Sudan Political Service, who was an eye-witness of the investiture of King Fafiti Yor, the twenty-ninth king, in 1918. However, the recent accounts by Mr Howell and Mr Thomson, who were able to make detailed observations on what happened on the death of King Fafiti Yor in 1943 and on the election and investiture of his successor, King Anei, in 1944 and again (Mr Thomson) on the death of King Anei and on the election and investiture of King Dak Fadiet in 1945, are descriptively fuller and analytically more illuminating and are therefore followed in the present summary.

On the death of a king his corpse is walled for some months in a hut and his bones are then buried in his natal hamlet, and not in the royal capital. The remains are disposed of, and the mortuary ceremonies conducted, by royal clients, *ororo*, and members of the royal clan (the head of which is not the ruling king but the chief of Fadiang settlement).

[1] P. Munro, 'Installation of the Ret of the Chol (King of the Shilluks)', *S.N. and R.* (1918).

It is more a clan, than a national, affair. The election of the new king, which takes place a few days after his predecessor's death, is, on the contrary, an affair of the whole Shilluk people, who participate in the election through the chiefs of the north and the south, to whom I have already referred.

These persons reflect in their roles in the election and in the ceremonies of investiture the structural dichotomy of Shillukland. We have seen that the Shilluk kingdom has a double configuration, political in its territorial setting, in its division into north and south and marches and settlements, and ritual in its religious setting, its arrangement in relation to the cult of Nyikang. In the ritual configuration the dichotomy is represented by the ceremonial division of the country into Gol Dhiang the northern division, and Gol Nyikang, the southern division, which correspond structurally to the political division of the kingdom into Ger, the northern half, and Luak, the southern half, though geographically they are not exactly coterminous. The chiefs of the ceremonial divisions in this ritual representation of the Shilluk polity are also the political chiefs of Golbany and Kwom, the two settlements which are to the north and south adjacent to the capital and cult-centre,

Fashoda, which is almost where the halves meet and is the focal point in the ceremonies of investiture.

I wish to emphasize that the procedure of election ensures that the prince selected to be king must have the backing of the whole country. Mr Thomson tells us that 'the choice rests entirely with the chiefs of Gol Dhiang and Gol Nyikang'[1] and cannot take place unless they agree, and it is clear that agreement does not depend on the personal feelings of the two men but that they are spokesmen for the halves of the country they represent. The other members of what Mr Howell and Mr Thomson call the 'electoral college' and which they say 'is a very conscious survival of the traditional structure of the Shilluk tribe'[2] have 'only to listen to the decision'[3] of these two men. The other members are the two influential chiefs of the northern and southern marches, Muomo and Tonga, nine chiefs of settlements who are descended from the original chiefs among whom Nyikang divided Shillukland when he conquered and settled his followers in it, and three important

[1] W. P. G. Thomson, 'Further Notes on the Death of a Reth of the Shilluk, 1945' (manuscript).
[2] *Op. cit.* p. 29.
[3] Thomson, *op. cit.*

24

chiefs of branches of the royal clan which have become dominant in powerful settlements in the country. Thus the backing, if only passive, of all parts of the kingdom is necessary before a prince can be invested with the kingship. The participation of the halves of Shillukland in the making of a king is further emphasized in the intense opposition between them expressed in the drama of the investiture, which at the same time enacts the conquest and settlement of the country by Nyikang and his followers.

Without the collective participation of the halves of the country the investiture of a king, which takes place about a year after his election, cannot be held. The ceremonies would seem to have precisely this function, for the kingship represents the whole country and a king can only be made by rites in which the whole country takes part. Hence also in the investiture all sections of the population are represented. The royal clan, its dispossessed branch, the commoner clans, especially those whose ancestors were among the original followers of Nyikang, and the client clans, all have essential roles in the drama. Different settlements in different districts of Shillukland and different clans are responsible for performing various parts of the ceremonial and for providing the various objects required in its enactment: silver and cloth from the Arabs of the north (presumably obtained by raiding in the old days), ostrich feathers for the effigies of Nyikang and his son, skins of the rare Mrs Gray antelope from Fanyikang island for the ceremonial robes of the king and the other more important participants in the ceremony, sacred spears, royal drums, fibre of the dom palm for ceremonial robes, cowrie shells, new huts, beasts for sacrifice, and so forth.

I will recount briefly the chief phases by which the kingship envelops the king-elect. The effigy of Nyikang, which is kept in the principal of his provincial shrines, at Akurwa in the most northerly district of Shillukland, is brought out by his priests, to whom the king-elect has to make considerable gifts for their service in this matter, and together with the effigy of his son Dak is taken to beat the northern bounds of the kingdom and then southwards, supported by an army of the north, to fight the king-elect for possession of the capital. As the effigies pass through each district the people gather to pay their respects to Nyikang and to escort him to the next district, for it appears that during the interregnum the effigy is believed to contain the spirit of Nyikang, to be Nyikang in fact. Nyikang's army of the north meets in mock combat an army of the south, supporting the king-elect, at the Arepejur watercourse just outside the royal capital. In the words of Mr Howell and Mr Thomson, this meeting in battle of the two armies on the Arepejur, the boundary between north and south, 'symbolizes the ceremonial division of the country into two moieties. The balance between them is strongly emphasized at all points.'[1] The army of the king-elect is defeated and he is captured by Nyikang and taken by him to the capital. The kingship captures the king. There Nyikang is placed on the royal stool. After a while he is taken off it and the king-elect sits on it in his stead and the spirit of Nyikang enters into him, causing him to tremble, and he becomes king, that is he becomes possessed by Nyikang. The concluding ritual acts follow. The new king has married a girl, traditionally provided by a certain clan, and this girl has an important role in the ceremonies of investiture. After the king's enthronement Nyikang seizes the girl and refuses to surrender her to the king on the ground that she was married with cattle from the royal herd, which is Nyikang's herd, and is therefore Nyikang's wife.

[1] *Op. cit.* p. 48.

On this issue Nyikang and the king summon their supporters to a second mock battle, in which the king captures the girl. Nyikang thereupon pays the king a visit to make his peace with him. On the following morning the king receives the homage and exhortations of the chiefs and undertakes to be a good king. Nyikang does not again contest the king's authority and some weeks later the effigies are sent back to the shrine at Akurwa.

Even so brief a sketch as I have given enables us to perceive the basic symbolism of the events of investiture. Nyikang is always king of the Shilluk and when a king dies his spirit is conceived of as departing in some manner from the king's body to take up its abode in the new effigy specially made for its accommodation at the shrine of Akurwa. By entering anew into the body of a prince Nyikang once again rules in his capital. The most adequate interpretation of the succession of rites of investiture would therefore seem to be that when the effigy and the king fight for possession of the capital the army of the effigy is victorious because Nyikang is in the effigy, but when they fight again over the king's bride the army of the king is victorious because Nyikang is now in the king. Power has passed from the Nyikang of the shrine of Akurwa to the Nyikang of the king in Fashoda. The king is now reverenced and the effigy is sent back to Akurwa.

It is Nyikang, mark you, the symbol of the whole Shilluk people, who is the king-maker. The king-ship belongs to all the people and not to the royal clan. Indeed, I think it significant that when Nyikang captures the king-elect the latter is ostenta-tiously surrounded by a block of his own clan. In this connection it is to be hoped that more will be learnt about the distribution now and in the past of the royal clan. The traditional home of Nyikang was Fanyikang, a settlement in the south, and the ritual equivalent to the southern half of the kingdom is Gol Nyikang. It seems likely on these, and on other, grounds that the royal clan was at one time found chiefly, perhaps only, in the south and spread from there to those northern settlements in which it is found to-day, as has happened among the closely related Anuak people. Hence in the ceremonies of investiture it seems as though the Shilluk people, represented by Nyikang and the army of the north, capture the king and take him away from his clan, represented by the army of the south, to be the head of the whole nation. The ritual of investiture appears to be an enactment of this central dogma, that it is not an individual who belongs to a particular clan or to a particular part of the country who is king, but Nyikang in whom are the continuity and welfare of the whole Shilluk people.

ROYAL SUCCESSION AND REGICIDE

We may now examine, in the light of what we have learnt about the position of the kingship in Shilluk society and particularly about the polarity so clearly expressed in the ceremonies I have reviewed, the mode of succession to royal office and the tradition of regicide which is so closely connected with it. Although Professor and Mrs Seligman say, 'We found no basis for the belief, common among Europeans in the Shilluk country, that there were two, or even three or four, branches of the royal house from which the kings were elected in turn',[1] the early *Sudan Intelligence Reports* make it clear that this was the case in recent decades and also that rivalry between claimants to the kingship in the second half of the nineteenth century was connected with the balanced opposition between north and south, for the halves of the kingdom fairly

[1] *Pagan Tribes of the Nilotic Sudan*, pp. 44–5.

consistently supported rival candidates. More-over, it is difficult to believe that the practice of the present day, by which it is more or less under-stood that the surviving lines of kings take it in turn to provide the king,[1] is new. A collateral royal line does not to-day contest an election on the understanding that they have next turn. The custom is for the reigning king to take under his wing a scion of a rival line and by so doing to in-dicate him as his successor, though he cannot nominate him and his choice may not be followed by the people. When this prince becomes king he takes under his wing a son of his protector. The reigning king insures by this convention against both rebellion by a rival line and his own line being excluded from the kingship in the future.

There can be no doubt that in recent times there has been an alternation on the throne of branches of the royal house, nor that the alternation is re-lated to the structural dichotomy of Shillukland. We are told that if the ceremonial chiefs of the north and south fail to reach agreement in the election of a new king the chiefs of the northern settlements follow their representative and the

[1] Westermann, *op. cit.* p. xlvi; Hofmayr, *op. cit.* p. 145; Howell and Thomson, *op. cit.* p. 27.

chiefs of the southern settlements follow their representative and the issue is fought out. It would seem probable that when there is disagreement it is an expression not of divergence of opinion about the merits of the candidates but of local loyalties in which different members of the royal house are associated with different parts of Shillukland. Whether disputed succession in the past was a product of local rivalries cannot perhaps now be determined, but it seems likely in view of the fact that in earlier times the king ruled from the settlement in which he was brought up or moved from one settlement to another and did not have a fixed residence at the central and neutral point of Fashoda.[1] I would also suggest that the association of princes with settlements and districts is clearly related to the custom by which they are brought up away from the capital. It is probable that the backing given by north and south to candidates for the kingship in past times arose from the fact that some princes were brought up in the north and some in the south. That this is the case is clear from Father Hofmayr's detailed notes on each of

[1] Seligman, *Report of the Wellcome Tropical Research Laboratories*, p. 229, citing information given by Father Banholzer and Dr Lambie; Westermann, *op. cit.* p. 138; Hofmayr, *op. cit.* p. 76.

the Shilluk kings.[1] It is easy to determine because the shrines of dead kings are still maintained to-day where they were born and brought up. I would further suggest that the maternal descent of princes may be of great significance in that it may be the association of maternal lineages with settlements which attaches local loyalties to a particular prince or to a particular branch of the royal house. It is therefore important that the maternal clans of the Shilluk kings should be recorded by some future observer.

The Shilluk statement that kings should be put to death if they grow old or become sick and their further statement that any prince may at any time challenge the king to mortal combat, in which the king may not call for help, cannot, I think, like the mode of succession, be understood except in relation to the political structure as a whole. There is only traditional evidence that any king has ever been killed in either way but, as Mr Howell and Mr Thomson point out,[2] the belief that kings have been, or might be, so killed has political implications. The assertion that a sick or old king should be killed probably means that when some disaster falls upon the Shilluk nation the tensions inherent

[1] *Op. cit.* pp. 59–136.   [2] *Op. cit.* p. 11.

in its political structure become manifest in the attribution of the disaster to his failing powers. The unpopularity which national misfortune brings on a king enables a prince to raise rebellion. The belief that a king may legitimately be assassinated by a personal rival is not substantiated by recent Shilluk history any more than the belief that he may be put to death, but it draws some support from tradition and from anxiety on this score shown by the king and his attendants and from the precautions he takes to protect himself against assassination, especially between his election and investiture and during the ceremonies of investiture. However, the evidence suggests that the anxiety may not be expressed, nor the precautions taken, solely on account of the king's feelings of insecurity but partly, if not chiefly, because he is compelled by tradition to act furtively. Moreover, it is difficult to reconcile the tradition that kings were killed in this fashion with the account we have of royal election and investiture. On the other hand there seems little doubt that Shilluk kings generally met a violent death. My own opinion is that we must interpret Shilluk statements about the matter as indicating not that any prince may slay the king on his own initiative, as has been suggested,[1] but that any prince may lead a rebellion as the candidate of discontent, particularly of the part of the kingdom to which the prince belongs. If the king has lost support in the part to which he belongs he will probably lose also both the resulting contest and his life in it. This is the conclusion I have drawn from Father Hofmayr's involved chronicle of the Shilluk kings.[2] It must here be remarked that Shilluk rebellions have not been made against the kingship. On the contrary, they were made to preserve the values embodied in the kingship which were being weakened, or it was believed so, by the individual who held office. They were not revolutions but rebellions against the king in the name of the kingship.

CONCLUSION

The divine kingship, to one, perhaps the best known, of the examples of which I have devoted this lecture, has been extensively written about by ethnologists, particularly in reference to its occur-

---

[1] Hofmayr, *op. cit.* p. 64; Prof. and Mrs Seligman, *Pagan Tribes of the Nilotic Sudan*, pp. 90–1. Howell and Thomson (*op. cit.* p. 11 *et passim*) are more reserved.

[2] *Op. cit.* pp. 59–136.

rence in Africa.[1] I cannot discuss their conclusions here though I feel that I must say about them that they are not, for me at any rate, well founded. In this lecture I thought that I could make a more valuable contribution by a detailed discussion of a particular instance than by what would necessarily have been a very general and superficial review of the whole field, especially as the case selected for discussion has been investigated by a number of gifted observers over half a century and still permits further and more systematic research.

In discussing the Shilluk kingship I have not, as you will have noted, followed Sir James Frazer's method of interpretation. In my view kingship everywhere and at all times has been in some degree a sacred office. *Rex est mixta persona cum sacerdote.* This is because a king symbolizes a whole society and must not be identified with any part of it. He must be in the society and yet stand outside it and this is only possible if his office is raised to a mystical plane. It is the kingship and not the king who is divine.

But though I would insist that a sufficient explana-

[1] Leo Frobenius, *Atlas Africanus*, Heft 2, Blatt 7, 'Der König ein Gott'; C. G. Seligman, *Egypt and Negro Africa* (the Frazer Lecture for 1933), 1934; Tor Irstam, *The King of Ganda. Studies in the Institutions of Sacral Kingship in Africa* (1944).

tion of the sacral kingship can only be derived from a detailed and painstaking comparative study of a wide range of monarchical institutions, which implies a yet wider comparative study of types of political structure, I do not wish to maintain that because all kingship has some of the features of the divine kingship the divine kingship is not in respect of other features a distinct type of institution. It is to the credit of Sir James Frazer to have shown that it is; and I would suggest that it is an institution typical of, though doubtless not restricted to, societies with pronounced lineage systems in which the political segments are parts of a loosely organized structure without governmental functions. In societies of this kind the political organization takes a ritual or symbolic form which in polities with a higher degree of organization gives way, though never entirely, to centralized administration.

I would further suggest that the acceptance of regicide in one form or another as customary can be explained in the same structural terms. The moral density is great enough for the segments to be represented by a common symbol in the kingship but not great enough to eliminate the powerful tendencies towards fission in the structure they compose. These tendencies are expressed in relation to the symbol, and either the kingship itself, or the king himself, circulates through the competitive segments, as among the Anuak and in past times also in Shillukland, or the segments struggle for royal representation in the capital. In either case their particularist sentiments operate through dynastic rivalries. The kingship, that is Nyikang, is changeless and acknowledged as a supreme value by all the Shilluk. In that permanence and in that acknowledgement the unity of the nation is manifested. In the rebellions against the kings and in the regicides the segmentary structure with its opposed local loyalties is equally present to the view of the observer. The kingship tends in such societies to become identified, by the attachment of the king's person to one locality, with sectional interests and when this happens other sections assert their rights, and by their action the common interest of all the Shilluk, in the kingship at the expense of the king's person. The kingship embodies a contradiction between dogma and social facts, in a sense between office and person, which is produced by a combination of centripetal and centrifugal tendencies in the national structure and this contradiction is solved by customary regicide.

BIBLIOGRAPHY

BANHOLZER, P. L. and GIFFEN, J. K. *The Anglo-Egyptian Sudan* (ed. Count Gleichen), ch. VIII. 1905.

CANN, CAPT. G. P. 'A Day in the Life of an idle Shilluk.' *S.N. and R.* 1929.

CRAZZOLARA, P. J. P. 'Beiträge zur Kenntnis der Religion und Zauberei bei den Schilluk.' *Anthropos.* 1932.

D.I. 'Conspiracy against the Mek of the Shilluks in 1917.' *S.N. and R.* 1922.

HOFMAYR, P. WILHELM. 'Zur Geschichte und sozialen und politischen Gliederung des Stammes der Schillukneger.' *Anthropos.* 1910.

HOFMAYR, P. WILHELM. 'Religion der Schilluk.' *Anthropos.* 1911.

HOFMAYR, P. WILHELM. *Die Schilluk. Geschichte, Religion und Leben eines Niloten-Stammes.* 1925.

HOWELL, P. P. 'The Shilluk Settlement.' *S.N. and R.* 1941.

HOWELL, P. P. and THOMSON, W. P. G. 'The Death of a Reth of the Shilluk and the Installation of his Successor.' *S.N. and R.* 1946.

MUNRO, P. 'Installation of the Ret of the Chol (King of the Shilluks).' *S.N. and R.* 1918.

OYLER, REV. D. S. 'Nikawng and the Shilluk Migration.' *S.N. and R.* 1918.

OYLER, REV. D. S. 'Nikawng's Place in the Shilluk Religion.' *S.N and R.* 1918.

OYLER, REV. D. S. 'The Shilluk's Belief in the Evil Eye. The Evil Medicine Man.' *S.N. and R.* 1919.

OYLER, REV. D. S. 'The Shilluk's Belief in the Good Medicine Men.' *S.N. and R.* 1920.

OYLER, REV. D. S. 'The Shilluk Peace Ceremony.' *S.N. and R.* 1920.

OYLER, REV. D. S. 'Shilluk Notes.' *S.N. and R.* 1926.

OYLER, MRS D. S. 'Examples of Shilluk Folk-Lore.' *S.N. and R.* 1919.

PUMPHREY, M. E. C. 'Shilluk "royal" Language Conventions.' *S.N. and R.* 1937.

PUMPHREY, M. E. C. 'The Shilluk Tribe.' *S.N. and R.* 1941.

SELIGMAN, PROFESSOR C. G. 'The Cult of Nyakang and the Divine Kings of the Shilluk.' *Report of the Wellcome Tropical Research Laboratories.* 1911.

SELIGMAN, PROFESSOR C. G. and MRS B. Z. *Pagan Tribes of the Nilotic Sudan*, chs. II and III. 1932.

TAPPI, P. C. 'Notes Ethnologiques sur les Chillouks.' *Bull. Soc. Khediv. de Géog.* 1903.

TAPPI, P. C. 'Le Pays des Chillouks.' *Bull. Soc. Khediv. de Géog.* 1904.

THOMSON, W. P. G. 'Further Notes on the Death of a Reth of the Shilluk, 1945.' (Manuscript.)

WESTERMANN, PROFESSOR DIEDRICH. *The Shilluk People, Their Language and Folklore.* 1912.

www.ingramcontent.com/pod-product-compliance
Ingram Content Group UK Ltd.
Pitfield, Milton Keynes, MK11 3LW, UK
UKHW042141280225
455719UK00001B/14

9 781107 678439